GREEN SPIRITUALITY

*Reflections on Belonging
To a World Beyond Myself*

VERONICA RAY

 HAZELDEN

Hazelden Educational Materials
Center City, Minnesota 55012-0176

ISBN: 0-89486-808-X

Editor's note
Hazelden Educational Materials offers a variety of information on
chemical dependency and related areas. Our publications do not
necessarily represent Hazelden's programs, nor do they officially speak
for any Twelve Step organization.

About the author
Veronica Ray is the author of several Hazelden titles, including
Choosing Happiness and the Moment to Reflect series on
Codependency, Spirituality, and Self-Esteem.

Design and illustrations by David Spohn

 The pages of this book are printed on recycled paper.

CONTENTS

INTRODUCTION vii

REFLECTIONS ON MY SELF 1

We all matter 2 • I nourish my body, mind, and spirit 3 •
What I do depends on how I see myself 4 • Living simply
frees me to live calmly, joyously, and compassionately 5 •
I don't always have to do things the way they've been done in
the past 6 • I see the world with awe and wonder 7 •
I contribute a positive mental attitude to the world's
consciousness 8 • I have a sacred place in nature 9 •
My mind is an important part of all that exists 10 • I am a
microcosm of the universe 11 • I give thanks for all my
blessings 12 • I look beyond the details of life 13 •
The world needs my contribution 14 • My peace and
serenity are untouched by the ups and downs of life 15 • My
outer expression reflects my true inner self 16 • I practice
mindfulness every day 17 • I use all forms of energy
efficiently 18 • I sing the song of life in harmony with the
whole world 19 • Our only true enemy is fear 20 •
Improvement is only possible through change and growth 21 •
Opposites can blend harmoniously into a new energy 22 •
I am a companion to all the animals on earth 23 •
The peace within me creates peace in the world 24 •
Everything I do has long-range effects 25 •

I will spend one whole day in mindfulness 26 • My spirit is present in everything I do 27 • I respect myself for the good of the world 28 • I conserve everything I use 29 • I recognize, respect, and nurture my ecological self 30 • I focus my energy on resolving the one true problem underlying all others 31 • I peacefully resist all the discouraging voices I hear 32 • I see the world through childlike eyes 33 • My choices and changes are important to the whole world 34 • I can always choose another point of view 35 • I take a moment every day to appreciate life 36 • The spiritual viewpoint always brings me back to my true self 37 • I am part of everything I see 38 • Today I will do one good thing for the world 39 • I don't need to "get back to nature," for it is always right here 40 • It's easy to live consciously, ethically, and lovingly 41 • My choices can change everything 42 • All the areas of my life are integrated into a harmonious whole 43 • In daily meditation, I feel my connection to all life 44

REFLECTIONS ON MYSELF AND OTHERS 45

The transformative relationship is a shared journey toward meaning 46 • I listen to my own true voice and that of others 47 • I love myself, other people, and all of life 48 • I have conscious relationships with everyone and everything 49 • All of my relationships are based on respect, courtesy, empathy, and equality 50 • Making amends for my mistakes is part of living in harmony with the rest of the world 51 • I am neither superior nor inferior to the rest of nature 52 • Human nature is good, honest, creative, intelligent, generous, harmless, helpful, kind, and peaceful 53 • My life is filled with heroes and helpers 54 • Listening is the beginning of true communication 55 •

I share in the world's joy 56 • For one day, I will do no harm
to any animal 57 • We share the natural world with all other
humans 58 • The more I learn about the world, the better my
interactions with it will be 59 • Thanksgiving is a natural part
of the cycle of life 60 • Our humanity transcends all our
differences 61 • I identify with all other living things 62 •
I will consciously cause no harm to others, the earth, or the
universe 63 • Compassion is the mark of true strength 64 •
Diversity is natural in the universe and in humanity 65

REFLECTIONS ON MYSELF AND MY COMMUNITIES 67

A good man is a public good 68 • I am a responsible
and important citizen of my country 69 •
I have pride in myself as a positive, contributing energy in the
universe 70 • The world is a complex and harmonious
network 71 • My life is an important and necessary part of the
world 72 • I live in society for the good of all 73 •
I belong to a changing variety of groups 74 • I have the
courage to follow my own inner values 75 • I am a conscious
and conscientious consumer 76 • Cooperation can benefit
all diverse people and groups 77 • I allow my identity to
grow 78 • Whatever happens to the world, happens
to me 79 • Whatever happens to me, happens to the
world 80 • I let go of blaming and focus on doing my part
to affect the world positively 81 • My work reflects one of
my best contributions to the world 82

REFLECTIONS ON MYSELF AND THE EARTH 83

Together with the sea, air, sunlight, and other life forms,
we take part in a planet-sized living system 84 •

Everything grows and evolves in cycles 85 • I am not a user of
the earth, but a responsible part of it 86 • Nature surrounds
me, wherever I am 87 • The earth nourishes me and keeps me
alive 88 • I listen to what the earth can teach me 89 •
Everything in nature has a purpose 90 • I am loyal to all life,
to the planet Earth, and to the universe 91 • The earth can
provide plenty for everyone 92 • I use my human power to
harmonize with and appreciate nature 93 • Nature provides
us with beautiful scents 94 • I see beauty everywhere in
nature 95 • The energy of the universe is infinite 96 •
Ecological imbalance is the result of human imbalance on a
personal and social level 97 • Nature fills me with
humility 98 • I am grateful for the gift of fire 99 • Water
sustains all life 100 • Music is a gift of nature 101 • Every
inch of space is part of the infinite living universe 102 •
Surrounded by nature, I feel my connection with it 103 •
Whatever we do to the earth, we do to ourselves 104 •
I close my eyes and imagine that I am a tree 105 • I take a
moment every day to remember my true place 106 • I value
all life in the universe 107 • I have a reciprocal relationship
with nature 108 • Nature is infinitely reliable 109 • I leave
the earth untouched as much as possible 110 • I can learn
from the plants and animals 111 • What is good for the
earth is good for me 112 • I am one with the whales of the
sea 113 • The energy of the universe is within me 114 •
I am part of healing the whole world 115 • I am like a
mountain 116 • I pledge allegiance to the earth… 117

INTRODUCTION

Methinks my own soul must be a bright invisible green.
—Henry David Thoreau

As we grow in our spiritual awareness, we evolve through many stages. Through self-examination, we learn a great deal about ourselves, our problems, behaviors, and motivations. Gradually, we begin turning our attention outward, to our relationships with other people, groups and communities, and ultimately, the whole world. We begin seeing ourselves as part of something much larger.

This new aspect of our self-identity is evidence of our growth and readiness to begin contributing more to the world around us. It's a natural step in the process of becoming more responsible human beings, connected to other people and a world beyond ourselves. When the spirit within us begins expressing itself outwardly, it does so in all of the relationships and communities in which we live. The harmony we have begun to feel within ourselves can now become harmony between us and the rest of the natural world.

Green spirituality combines our ecological and spiritual mindfulness. It's a relationship with everything around us, based on the recognition of ourselves, other people, nature, and the universe as sacred expressions of divine energy. We don't usually use words like "divine" or "sacred" to describe nature or even ourselves, but the interconnectedness of all life is truly a miraculous harmony.

We humans have inhabited the earth for only a tiny fraction of its existence. Yet, in that time, we have learned to harness its energies and utilize its resources for an amazingly wide variety of purposes. We have learned to use the land, water, animal and vegetable life, minerals, and atmosphere for our survival, comfort, and pleasure. We have also created weapons of destruction and disrupted the natural balances of our earth to a dangerous degree. If we continue in this manner, we will either destroy ourselves or create a world unfit for human habitation.

But this frightening scenario doesn't have to be. *We're so much better than this.* The problem is *not* that we love ourselves at the expense of other people, other species, and nature, but rather that we *don't* love ourselves enough to know who we truly are and what we truly need. We don't recognize that our own well-being is intimately entwined with the well-being of all people and the entire earth, and that we become truly safe and happy by flowing harmoniously with the river of all life rather than trying to conquer and control it.

Humanity is suffering from low self-esteem, self-worth, and self-confidence. We don't seem to know how truly wonderful we are, how great we can be. We're like children in a classroom who have been told they will fail, that they aren't capable of anything else—we're living out what we believe about ourselves. We act as if we don't have the amazing and unique capacities that we possess. We ignore what we have intuitively known all along—that we are an important and integral part of a glorious life system, the consciousness of the universe, the children who *can* succeed.

We are living in a time of great revelation and revolution. Changing knowledge and insight create changing beliefs, attitudes, choices, and ultimate effects. The marriage of science and human insight, *intuition*, or *spirituality* can now move us into a new stage of growth, fulfilling our potential in our rightful place in the universe. Beginning with our personal relationships with ourselves and others, and moving out into ever-widening communities, we can exercise our new self-image as a wonderfully powerful force, pulsing in harmony with the natural rhythms of the whole universe. We can reevaluate our past, make amends for our mistakes, and move forward with newfound wisdom.

REFLECTIONS
ON
MY SELF

We all matter. Every one of us has an essential contribution to make, and we can do so only by taking the risk of being uniquely our own selves.

—Carol S. Pearson

As we grow in knowledge and understanding of ourselves, we discover our unique abilities and opportunities for self-expression. We find the validity of our own experience, viewpoint, and talents. Even our particular difficulties and flaws can be seen as special challenges for growth.

The insight we gain into our true selves reveals our similarity and interconnectedness to all others. We are each an important part of many larger systems. Discovering our part and the contribution we can make grows out of an inner quest for self-discovery. As Duane Elgin writes in *Voluntary Simplicity,* "We cannot expect there to be peace within the human family if we are at war within ourselves." Inner harmony and peace within ourselves enable us to share these same qualities with others and the world. It all begins within each one of us.

I nourish my body, mind, and spirit.

Our bodies are part of the natural world. But, too often, we may think of them as machines. Even if we give them enough fuel in the form of food, we may expect them to run smoothly without adequate rest and relaxation, or mental, emotional, and spiritual nourishment.

Beauty, periods of silence, music, laughter, and peaceful, joyful, harmonious companionship are as essential to our health as food, water, air, sunshine, and exercise. In the wild, other mammals are serenaded by streams and waterfalls, rustling leaves, birds singing, and crickets chirping. Dairy farmers increase their milk yield by playing soothing music for the cows. Babies smile at beautiful pictures. We don't need to be "educated" about beautiful sights, sounds, and feelings—we just need to let ourselves enjoy them naturally. Our bodies respond to our minds, hearts, and spirits.

What I do depends on how I see myself.

If we see ourselves as small, insignificant individuals, unconnected to other people and communities, that is how we will behave. If we don't value our consciousness as a unique gift, we won't use it to infuse our choices with ethics and values. If we don't believe we matter, how will we ever believe in the value of all people, animals, the earth, and the universe?

Developing a positive self-image means much more than realizing that we're good enough to live in this world and to live well. It means recognizing the amazing, wonderful, beautiful, even *sacred* reality of being human. It means recognizing our place in our families and other groups, our communities, all of humanity, all life on the earth, and everything in the universe. Our choices and actions can reflect that we are each important and valuable.

Living simply frees me to live calmly, joyously, and compassionately.

While most of us agree that our lives have become cluttered with material objects and stresses, we may still avoid the call to live more simply. We may fear that living simply means some sort of self-imposed poverty, austerity, or suffering. We may fear losing the busyness and material things that we hope will bring us happiness—even when we know they won't. We may not know what else to do.

Living simply means letting go of all those unnecessary attachments to activities and things. Unlike poverty, simplicity is a *choice*, a decision to live our lives focused on what truly matters. It's a decision to spend our time, energy, and money *consciously*, and that requires a little thought about our real values and priorities. Living simply frees us to enjoy true happiness.

I don't always have to do things the way they've been done in the past.

Sometimes doing the best thing, based on a consciousness of the consequences for all, means doing things in new ways. When we examine our choices, free of old assumptions and thought patterns, we can discover new possibilities and improvements. Every day, if we let ourselves, we can learn new things and expand our point of view. Old choices were based on old viewpoints and previous levels of knowledge and understanding. Our new choices can reflect our growing awareness of the critical part we each play on this earth.

We don't have to feel threatened by the possibility of replacing some of our old habits with new choices. In the past, we did the best we could with what we knew and believed. Now, we can let go of the security of old ways and let our new understanding lead us to a better future than we ever dreamed possible.

I see the world with awe and wonder.

Everything is a miracle. We are surrounded by and filled with miraculous events. Giant oaks grow from tiny acorns; birds migrate with the changing seasons; people learn to speak, read, and write; the gravitational pull of the sun, moon, and all the planets keeps them where they are in relation to one another. . . . The universe is an awesome, wondrous miracle.

When we lose touch with the awe and wonder of life, we also lose touch with ourselves. We forget who we are in this vast universe. We become confused and start making mistakes.

Take a moment to remember where you are and who you are. Look at the moon and stars. Feel the wind, rain, and snow. Stand by quietly and watch the children, the animals, the flowers, and the tides. Listen to the birds, the rushing water, the whales, and the thunder. Be very still and remember the awe and wonder of it all.

I contribute a positive mental attitude to the world's consciousness.

It's so easy to become depressed, discouraged, angry, and tired of life. There's so much misery, poverty, hunger, homelessness, disease, disharmony, ignorance, and violence. Negativity may seem the only possible viewpoint, our anger justified, our hopelessness realistic. But do these attitudes contribute to solving problems or relieving human suffering?

Whether we realize it or not, we always have a choice as to how we respond to any circumstance. Often, it seems we respond with blame and inertia. We believe the problems are too big and we are too small to do anything. A world full of such hopelessness can never survive. But we still have the choice. We can do what we can, give what we have, and hope for the best. Our own efforts can join with those of others to change the world.

I have a sacred place in nature.

We can develop a personal relationship with the natural world. Whether we live in the country, city, or suburbs, we can all change our relationship with nature by creating a sacred place for ourselves. The sacred place can be a tree, rock, beach, field, park, flower or vegetable garden, or a small patch of grass or weeds. It doesn't matter how large or elaborate it is as long as it's part of the natural world.

Look at your sacred place. Be still and listen to it. Watch it closely. Go to it in sunshine, rain, cold, heat, morning dew, high noon, and all seasons. Notice its colors, textures, and changes. Touch it, see what it sees, and feel what it feels. Get to know it as you know your best friend. Your sacred place is nature's gift to you.

My mind is an important part of all that exists.

Ecologist and theologian Thomas Berry writes that the earth is made up of five major components: the geology or land, the water, the atmosphere, the biological life, and consciousness—*the mind*. While we argue over how to use, protect, and maintain the first four components, how much attention do we each give to the last one?

Our minds—our thoughts, knowledge, and beliefs—have a tremendous impact on the world. The earth evolved and maintained itself for billions of years before we humans started affecting it with our choices. Now it is in our hands. We can harmonize with the earth's natural rhythms or treat it with ignorance and abuse. Every one of us contributes to the earth's overall consciousness.

I am a microcosm of the universe.

Everything in the universe is a reflection of something in ourselves: the cycles of birth, growth, and death; the unconscious rhythm of life-sustaining forces; the unity of diverse parts working together as a whole. The universe also reflects our inner struggles, our self-image, beliefs, and feelings. Conflicts within our hearts become conflicts in all our relationships.

Harmony doesn't mean there are no conflicts. It does mean resolving conflicts constructively and patiently. We can respond with openness and understanding rather than fear and domination. When we begin making peace within, all our relationships will become more peaceful and productive.

I give thanks for all my blessings.

We receive so much from other people, the earth, and the universe. The sun shines and the rain falls on us all, indiscriminately. The air is free for everyone, the stars a nightly visual feast. The earth brings forth all kinds of food and raw materials for our use, comfort, and pleasure. The trees give us fruit and nuts, shade from the hot sun, and wood for our homes and furniture. They don't care who we are or what we do; they're always completely generous.

We often neglect to notice the gifts we also receive from other people: the expertise and care of doctors, nurses, and teachers; the skill of construction workers, mechanics, and technical experts of all kinds; the toil of farmers, shippers, and grocery store workers. Everywhere we look there are products and services for which to be thankful.

I look beyond the details of life.

Our everyday lives are cluttered with superficial things. These details are like weeds—easily taking over, obscuring our focus on what really matters. Caught up in a constant barrage of details, we often lose touch with ourselves, other people, and our true place in the world.

The details of life can separate us from others, give us false identities, and distract us from learning, sharing, teaching, growing, and helping each other. They keep our attention on things that don't really matter to avoid facing and dealing with the things that do.

We don't have to accept these details at face value. We can question every assumption we've ever made. We can deliberately look at everything in a different way. We can let the details of our lives fall away and see what's really going on, maybe for the very first time.

The world needs my contribution.

Each one of us is a unique expression of life. We have a variety of talents and opportunities. We each bring something special to the world; without us, the world would be different. Understanding that about ourselves helps us consciously contribute all that we can.

There is an old Native American thanksgiving custom where everyone brings something and places it on an altar to give, then they take something away for themselves. This is the way the world works—constantly circulating gifts of all life forms, continuously giving and receiving. We are part of that flow. If we don't know what we have to offer, if we don't bring our gifts, something irreplaceable is missing.

My peace and serenity are untouched
by the ups and downs of life.

While growing through many stages and experiences, we learn that ups and downs are inevitable. We also learn we can face up to them, live through them, and learn from them. The old saying *This too shall pass* begins to have meaning as we ourselves experience it. Ups and downs follow one another as day follows night and spring follows winter.

Maintaining our equilibrium takes patience, hope, and trust. It means accepting that there can't be mountains without valleys, yes without no, *yin* without *yang*. This natural flow of opposing energies is always present through personal lives and relationships, growth of communities and nations, evolution of humanity, and all life. Disruption can be turned into the light of a new day.

My outer expression reflects my true inner self.

The way we learn to use language, both verbal and non-verbal, is strongly influenced by our environment. We learn early to lie, intimidate, manipulate, or pretend; to be coy, vulgar, sincere, or rude; to speak softly, clearly, loudly, or to mumble. Throughout our lives, our speech and other forms of expression change as our surroundings do. We conform to language habits of those we want to be with, and we feel frustrated when people make incorrect assumptions about us based on our old habits of self-expression.

Consciously choosing how we will express ourselves verbally and in every other way can help us present ourselves more accurately to others. It can help us communicate honestly rather than trying to impress or manipulate people. It can make us feel more comfortable with our own bodies, voices, and words, and can improve all our relationships.

I practice mindfulness every day.

Mindfulness has two components: reminding ourselves to be aware of our values and responsibilities, and exercising that awareness in our actions and interactions. Being mindful means thinking about everything we do: Why are we doing it? What are the effects? Simply being aware of ourselves and our surroundings we can note: Where are we? What are the elements in our environment and how are we affecting them?

Sometimes we need to just close our eyes and become aware of our breathing. Or, we can look very closely at a tree, flower, rock, kitten, or color. Sometimes we need to be very still and listen to a bird, a rain shower, or another person. These exercises in mindfulness bring us back to our true selves, to our inner truth.

I use all forms of energy efficiently.

There are many forms of energy—gravity, growth, decay—and transformations of everything from matter to human emotions and behaviors. Thomas Berry, an ecologist and theologian, has called the entire universe an "energy event."

Using energy efficiently simply means using it for specific purposes without waste. When we walk, we don't flail our arms about or shake our head back and forth; our arms, legs, and entire body work together in one smooth motion to keep us going forward. Likewise, when one lamp will light a room, we don't need to turn on five. Using all the forms of energy in the world conservatively and efficiently makes everything we do more effective and frees us from having to spend more energy later trying to fix our mistakes and clean up our messes.

I sing the song of life in harmony with the whole world.

The song of life vibrates throughout the universe, each instrument of the vast orchestra playing its unique, necessary part. Each species lends its voice to the ensemble. Every range, from soprano to bass, fills out the infinite choir.

When one section of the orchestra loses its timing, or plays when it should be silent, or remains silent when it should play, the whole symphony falls into discord. When humanity tries to sing without listening to the others, the whole world falls into disharmony.

But we can learn to harmonize with all other life forms, the earth, and the universe. Instead of throwing the whole song off key, we can learn to blend in perfect harmony.

Our only true enemy is fear.

What stops us from being our compassionate, giving, sharing, peaceful selves? Why do we maintain attitudes and behaviors we know to be harmful? What keeps us locked in our defensive little worlds rather than recognizing our intimate connections to all other things? The answer is *fear*.

Fear blocks us from expressing our true natures. It makes us feel alone in a hostile universe. It offers us separation, domination, jealousy, envy, defensiveness, and hate as ways of coping with the world. But what alternatives do we have? Truth, love, peace, community, compassion, contemplation, cooperation, gratitude, responsibility, and *risk*. We already know what fear does; why not take a chance on fearlessness?

Improvement is only possible through change and growth.

While it is a natural and common phenomenon, change is often difficult for us to accept. While we may agree that old ways of doing things have produced problems, we may resist letting go of those familiar patterns. While we say our beliefs have changed, our behaviors may continue along well-worn lines.

Resistance to change is a peculiarly human trait. It grows out of the fearfulness of our egocentric self-image, our defensive desire to stay on top of some imagined hierarchy of life. Change is only threatening if we imagine ourselves to be the controllers of the universe. But the universe has natural laws, and we can either learn to live with them or uselessly try to dominate them. Letting go of our imagined control, we can become a naturally harmonious—and ever-changing—part of life.

Opposites can blend harmoniously into a new energy.

We are so used to thinking *dualistically* that we tend to immediately choose sides of any problem or issue. We think that either *this* or *that* is the only way to look at the situation; that if something is true, its opposite must be false; that one side must win and the other must lose.

But there is another way of looking at conflicts and problems. If we view them *dialectically* rather than *dualistically*, then both *this* and *that* can be true, right, or chosen. A *dialectic* is a synthesis of both sides so that a new view or choice can be formed. Dualism polarizes. There can be no compromise or harmony possible in a dualistic viewpoint.

Choosing to think dialectically, we can see new ways of resolving problems. When no one has to lose, we can *all* win.

I am a companion to all the animals on earth.

Many of us have had personal relationships with some kind of animal—dogs, cats, horses, parakeets, or house pets of some kind. Most of us have visited the zoo, or lived on a farm, or watched the birds and squirrels in a park. Some of us have seen dolphins and whales playing in the ocean or heard wolves howling to one another from their mountaintops.

When our relationships with animal life have been respectful, peaceful, and kind, they have given us joy. When these relationships have been fearful, aggressive, or unkind, they have harmed us. We are spiritually related to all nonhuman life, as we are related to one another. The love and companionship we share with others of the earth returns to us.

The peace within me creates peace in the world.

Whether peace is our goal in our personal relationships; or between our political, religious, social, or ethnic groups; or between our nations; or between human and all other life, it always begins inside *us*.

Facing the conflicts within us reveals the differences between our outer behaviors and our inner truth. When we act in ways that seem advantageous but go against our values, we hurt ourselves and others. Justifying the choices that can cause harm doesn't convince us on a deep level that they're right. When we let our true inner selves guide our actions, we can begin creating similar harmony outside of ourselves.

Everything I do has long-range effects.

When we make our day-to-day decisions, how often do we think about their consequences far into the future? Native American custom teaches us to consider effects of any action on *seven generations* to come, but how many of us can imagine *seven generations* ahead? How often do we even consider the effects our choices may have next week or next year?

The further we are able to imagine into the future, the better we will be able to contribute positively to it. When we buy anything, we can look at its packaging: What will happen to it when we throw it away? What about its usefulness: Can it be used for several years or for only a short time? What will we do when it's used up? What alternatives to buying it do we have? When we decide to say or do something, we can ask similar questions: Who might be affected, how, and for how long? We can remember our choices always have far-reaching effects.

I will spend one whole day in mindfulness.

For just one day in a lifetime of many thousands of days, we can become conscious of our environments and all our choices. When we get up, we can think about the warmth of the air we breathe, the clothes we wear, and the place where we live. Turning on the tap, we can recognize the life-giving water we usually take for granted. Eating, we can think about the natural sources of all our nourishment. Driving to work, we can think about gasoline, air pollution, carpooling, or alternative transportation. Putting out the trash, we can think about where it will go. Turning on our lights, we can think about electricity and energy conservation. Shopping, we can think about the social responsibilities of manufacturers, sellers, and consumers.

Just one day of mindfulness can open our eyes, hearts, and minds to our true place in all our communities and the world. It can be a day of making new decisions, a day of consciousness and revelation, a day that will change the rest of our lives.

My spirit is present in everything I do.

We often think our spirituality is totally separate from everything else. We may believe it has a place one day a week in one area of our lives. We may wonder how it could possibly have anything to do with our political, social, or practical choices. We may think it is as far away from our relationship and interaction with the earth as anything can be.

But our spirit is always present, in everything we do. When we take a spiritual viewpoint, our choices become harmonious, harmless, and helpful to life as a whole. Our spirituality manifests itself lovingly and generously in the world. It can change every facet of our daily lives, leading us to accept the things we can't change and make the greatest contribution to the things we can change. The spirit in us can connect with the spirit in all other people, animals, and nature in a harmonious dance of life.

I respect myself for the good of the world.

We are all human beings deserving and *needing* respect for our integrity, dignity, feelings, and rights. We require the respect of others, but more importantly, of ourselves. Without the self-respect that keeps us from harming our bodies, minds, feelings, and lives, we can't get the respect of others.

When we recognize the interconnectedness of all life, we see that we are affected by the harm done to others, and others are affected by harm done to us. Our responsibility to the world includes responsibility to ourselves. Taking care of ourselves in the truest, best sense means not allowing or contributing to our own harm. It means making choices that reflect true self-respect.

I conserve everything I use.

Conservation doesn't mean self-sacrifice or deprivation. It simply means not *wasting* the things we use. It means being mindful of where things come from and where they go after we use them. It means being a harmless, harmonious part of the continuous cycle of life on earth.

Aldo Leopold writes, "Conservation is a state of harmony between men and land." We live on, off, and with the land, air, water, plants, and animals. We interact and interexist with them. To be *conservative* in our connecting to other elements of life is to respect their place here too. The underlying truth is clear and simple: We are part of the earth, and the earth is part of us.

I recognize, respect, and nurture my ecological self.

There are many "selves" to who we are. Based on gender, ethnicity, nationality, and race, we have specific identities. Our roles in our families and workplaces, and our political, religious, and philosophical groups, create other "selves." We each have many endings for the phrase, "I am . . . " Growing up means examining and defining these various elements of our self-image.

Our ecological self comes through recognizing our spirituality and how all life is interconnected. We realize that we fit into a vast web of humans, animals, plants, and the universe. We are an integral part of one great living system. This ecological and spiritual self-identity reminds us of our responsibilities for living harmoniously with all life on earth.

I focus my energy on resolving the one true problem underlying all others.

Sometimes it's difficult for us to see the connection between the earth's fate and our own. It may seem foolish to be concerned about the treatment of animals while humans still suffer from hunger, poverty, disease, and violence. There may seem to be so many problems that it's almost impossible to prioritize them.

But just as we are all interconnected, our social problems are too. They all grow out of the same underlying mistake in the way we view life. The same error in thinking that leads us to mistreat animals can also lead us to mistreat ourselves and each other. And it's the same mistaken belief that creates war and environmental disaster. What is this mistake? It's our collective low self-worth, our lack of faith in the basic goodness of humanity, our delusion that some must suffer so that others can prosper. Focusing our energy on this problem can help us resolve other problems.

I peacefully resist all the discouraging voices I hear.

Our lives and our minds are often full of voices telling us what we *can't* do and who we *can't* be. There never seems to be a shortage of reasons why we *shouldn't* try new things, take risks, or do our best. There are always plenty of negative blocks to our realizing our highest dreams and goals.

It's very easy to fall in line with discouraging voices. We do it because we're afraid of failure, success, or the unknown. We do it to try to gain other people's approval or to belong to the crowd. And all the while we know deep inside that we're capable of so much more.

When we stop allowing the negative voices to stop us, we begin to discover just how wonderful we can be, how wonderful life can be. When we peacefully resist all the discouragement, we find the courage within ourselves to be what we can be and do what we can do. And that's why we're here.

I see the world through childlike eyes.

When we were children, we rolled down grassy hills and climbed tall trees. We felt the sand between our toes on the beach and noticed the changing moon in the night sky. Everything was new, fascinating, and beautiful to us. But as adults, we rarely see all the interesting, glorious things our world is made of. We stopped noticing the beauty and wonder of nature, focusing all our attention on our own lives and problems.

One of the most wonderful things about being around children is that on occasion, we can see nature through their eyes. Once again, the world looks fresh and new. But we don't need to wait for those special moments when we're around children. We can reawaken the child within ourselves and see the world through that child's eyes here and now.

My choices and changes are important to the whole world.

It's so easy to feel small and insignificant. So often, we sink into depression, boredom, and fatalism. We think nothing we do matters, that we can't make a difference. But we are each part of larger systems and communities. We individually contribute our attitudes, beliefs, actions, and choices to all of these groups. We individually have a much greater effect than we know.

All big, collective changes are made up of many small, individual changes. We don't have to wait for everyone else to change before we do. We can lead the way, make a small difference, begin to light the path.

I can always choose another point of view.

Sometimes we get stuck in one viewpoint and can't see any other. We think a problem has no solution, that change is impossible. We close our minds to new information or different perspectives. We give up trying to communicate, compromise, or cooperate with other people. We may not even realize that the only block to resolution and change is our own stubborn point of view.

Just because we've always believed something doesn't mean that it's true or that believing it is good for us. Just because other people believe something doesn't necessarily mean we have to. Something that used to be true won't always be in the future. Open-mindedness keeps us from getting stuck in old ways.

I take a moment every day to appreciate life.

There's nothing like getting sick once in a while to make us appreciate feeling well. Likewise, times of lack and difficulty help us value the happier, more abundant times in our lives. But when do we get a reminder to appreciate life itself? People who have come close to death often say it changes their perspective completely. But by the time most of us face death, it's too late to start appreciating life.

We don't need to survive a heart attack or a car accident, or be diagnosed with a terminal illness, to begin appreciating the gift of life. We can do it right now and every day of our lives. It only takes a moment's awareness of the energy within us. It just means remembering the value of our own existence.

The spiritual viewpoint always brings me back to my true self.

Whenever we ask ourselves, *What is the spiritual point of view here?* we see everything differently. We can open up to our true nature and our place in the world. We can feel our spiritual connection to all other living things. The spiritual viewpoint reminds us of what we are capable of accomplishing.

With a spiritual point of view, we can look at every question, choice, and decision—every aspect of ourselves and our lives—with fresh eyes. We can let go of our fear and defensiveness and see the good within everything and everyone. We can see the possibilities for improvement where we may have given up. With a spiritual outlook, we can see the forest *and* the trees.

I am part of everything I see.

Author D. H. Lawrence wrote, "I am part of the sun as my eye is part of me." Just as every cell in our body is part of us, we—along with everything else—are like cells in the body of the earth.

If we remember that we are part of a larger whole, it can change the way we interact with all kinds of events, circumstances, and objects. When things break down or go wrong, we can think, *I am one with this,* and we can imagine how to heal ourselves rather than feeling angry and stuck. We can feel music and poetry enter into our minds and hearts, not just our ears. We can feel our oneness with people, animals, and plants, and develop a spiritual relationship with them.

Today I will do one good thing for the world.

We often neglect to do all we can simply because we forget our power to affect things. We don't realize all the good we're capable of contributing, or we don't believe our contribution is important. We may feel too busy, stressed, sad, angry, or tired to think about doing anything for the world.

An old saying reminds us that we shall only pass this way once and should do whatever good we can here and now, for we won't get a second chance. But we may think we'll have many more chances to do good—to speak kindly to someone, to offer our help, to give something away. We may believe that one careless act today won't matter, as long as we don't do it every day. But *today is the only today we'll ever have*. Let's use it to do one good thing.

I don't need to "get back to nature," for it is always right here.

Many of us live in areas where there is more concrete than soil, more manicured landscapes than wild forests or prairies. We may think that nature is something we have to "get back to" out in the country somewhere. We may believe it's a nice romantic idea, but not relevant to our busy lives. We may think that there are people who are *into* nature, and people who aren't—and we aren't.

But our relationship with nature isn't something we necessarily have to find out in the wilderness. It's a point of view, a state of mind, a sense of *self*. We *are* nature. It is above, below, all around, and running through us. Our relationship with nature is found within our hearts and souls.

It's easy to live consciously, ethically, and lovingly.

Sometimes we think it's just too much trouble to think about everything we do and how it affects everything else. We believe that learning about people, plants, animals, the earth, and the universe requires a lot of schooling, or that choosing products and actions that are good for the world would be expensive or self-sacrificing.

But it really can be easy, economical, and pleasant to live consciously and harmlessly. The information we need is readily available to all of us, and alternative products are now abundant in the marketplace. Recycling and filling our homes with products that are good for us and the environment make us feel good; not buying things that cause harm has a cleansing effect on our outlook. Thinking about the effects of our choices quickly becomes a habit that benefits us and others.

My choices can change everything.

We make so many choices every day of our lives. When we get up in the morning, we choose our toothpaste and soap, the clothes we will wear, the food we will eat for breakfast. We choose our transportation and the kind of work we do. We constantly make choices about the things we think, say, and do.

These choices have far-reaching effects. Becoming aware of our choices rather than letting them remain mindless habits can make their effects more positive. First, we can ask ourselves if we are being *harmless*. Then, we can think about how we might be *helpful*. These two questions can help bring us back to our best possible choices. All our choices are important enough to *think* about.

All the areas of my life are integrated into a harmonious whole.

There are many aspects to our lives—family, work, hobbies and recreation, religion, ethics. Together they make up who we are. Whenever they are not in harmony, we feel confused, upset, or angry. We can't function at our best unless all our parts are working together.

For instance, if we neglect our families for the sake of our jobs, both suffer, and we feel an unpleasant pull in both directions. If our actions do not reflect our ethics, we feel discontent. Integrating all the aspects of ourselves in harmony creates peace within us. Then, we can begin creating peace outside ourselves.

In daily meditation, I feel my connection to all life.

When we take a few moments each day to let go of our busy thoughts and worries, we can remember who we really are. We can relax into our true selves, feeling our oneness with all other people, plant and animal life, the earth, and the whole universe. We can spend a little time with our deepest souls, our highest sense of being.

We can spend this time thinking about the natural world, imagining ourselves in various places, one with birds, fishes, and trees. Or we can think about the whole planet, spinning and flying through space, one of many, pulling and pushing one another in a harmonious pattern of life. We can imagine a great net, connecting all things and beings together, each part affecting the rest. We can open our minds to the spirit within ourselves, and feel our connection to the spirit of all living things.

REFLECTIONS
ON
MYSELF
& OTHERS

The transformative relationship is a shared journey toward meaning.

—Marilyn Ferguson

Our relationships with other people are the first steps out of ourselves and into the world. Every relationship that touches our lives presents us with opportunities for learning and adding something to the lives of others.

As we recognize our interconnectedness with other people, we begin seeing the far-reaching effects of what we do. A smile freely given, a loving word spoken or an angry one held back—these are the simple ways we make powerful differences in others' lives.

Together, we journey toward finding and understanding the meaning in our lives. Together, we discover that we are not so different from one another. Together, we find the strength and support that none of us has alone.

Whether or not we recognize it, we are responsible, one to another. We affect each other profoundly, every day of our lives. When we consciously and deliberately take responsibility for ourselves in relation to others, we can transform ourselves, our relationships, and, ultimately, the world.

I listen to my own true voice and that of others.

Sometimes we get so wrapped up in trying to please or impress others or defend ourselves against them that we lose touch with ourselves and one another. We forget our hurt feelings by covering them up with anger; we suppress our fear of rejection and pretend we don't care. We do the same thing when listening to other people—reacting to words or behaviors and ignoring their real, true inner meaning.

But inside each one of us, the truth remains. Behind all the games and pretenses, underneath all the silences and phoniness, our real voice still whispers. When we listen beyond, "I don't care," we can start hearing, "Please help me." When we stop trying to protect ourselves from being hurt, and simply say, "I'm hurt," we can open up true communication with others. The real part of us can connect with the real part of them only when we listen to our hearts, and theirs.

I love myself, other people, and all of life.

What does it mean to *love* a person or another living thing? It means recognizing its true nature and accepting its value and sacredness. It means consciously causing it no harm and actively making reparations when harm has inadvertently been done. It means empathizing with it, sharing its joy, pain, sorrow, and recognizing its needs. It means leaving it alone to grow through its own cycles and contributing what we can to its well-being.

To love, in this sense, is to respect, honor, and nurture. We recognize the beauty in those we love, and appreciate their contributions to our lives and well-being, but we don't possess them. They are not ours to own, use, or abuse, but rather are gifts we are privileged to know. Loving ourselves and other living things in this way can heal us all.

I have conscious relationships with everyone and everything.

Having *conscious* relationships means being aware of the effects we have. How do our habits of eating and drinking, using electricity, water, and fuels, or traveling, working, playing, and living affect the rest of the world? How do our words and actions affect other people? What kinds of ripples are we creating on the sea of life?

Becoming conscious of all our relationships can help us to make more responsible and positive choices. Thinking of ourselves *in relationship* to the animals, fish, and plant life and the very earth from which we get our homes, cars, clothes, and food can remind us of our constant interaction with the whole planet and universe. If we become as conscious in all our relationships as we try to be in our special human relationships, we can avoid causing harm and can make our impact a good one.

All of my relationships are based on respect, courtesy, empathy, and equality.

The relationships we have with ourselves, other people, animals, and nature all require our attention. While they are all different, they all still need respect, courtesy, empathy, and equality for health and harmony.

We respect people, animals, and nature by recognizing them as they are and valuing their right to be who and what they are. We courteously refrain from treating them harmfully or carelessly. We empathize with them by trying to see things from their viewpoint, even if it is very different from ours.

Equality in our relationships means all people are equally valuable. While parents have greater responsibilities than children, children and parents have equal importance within a family. Likewise, humans are equal to other living things. When we treat *all* of our relationships with the same respect, courtesy, empathy, and equality, we all become part of a harmonious whole.

*Making amends for my mistakes is part of living in harmony
with the rest of the world.*

Not one of us is perfect. We all make mistakes, sometimes even causing harm. As we learn to live consciously, to think about the effects of all our choices on the
rest of the world, we discover the necessity and power of
making amends.

Admitting our errors, apologizing for them, and making
whatever restitution we can enables us to move forward
free of old burdens of guilt. It helps us learn the lesson
within the error and avoid making similar mistakes in the
future. It keeps us learning and improving our impact on
humanity and the earth.

It also reminds us that we are imperfect human beings,
like everybody else. That realization can bring us closer to
others and help us to remember our interconnectedness
with all other people. We are all in this together.

I am neither superior nor inferior to the rest of nature.

Feeling superior to the rest of nature, humankind has nearly destroyed it. Feeling small and inferior to the vast and awesome wonder of the universe, we could easily resign ourselves to our worst faults. In either case, we are not able to live up to our potential as a powerful part of one harmonious life force.

A new attitude of equality, cooperation, and mutuality between ourselves and all others can change our own lives and the whole world. We can begin to see our true role as unique and important beings in a vast interconnected system of many unique and important beings.

Human nature is good, honest, creative, intelligent, generous, harmless, helpful, kind, and peaceful.

The term *human nature* has been used to explain, justify, defend, and excuse every kind of harm of which we are capable. The *law of the jungle* and *survival of the fittest* have become mottos for condoning the worst in us. If we don't survive our own environmental abuse or nuclear inventions, it will be because we simply didn't use our better qualities to their fullest.

Human nature includes one unique element: *choice*. When an animal is hungry, it uses instinct to find its food. We humans can choose from a wide variety of farming, fishing, and animal sources for our food. We can choose *how* to grow our food and *how much* to grow. We can choose how to treat the animals we keep for food. We can exercise the *choice* of human nature for the good of all life.

My life is filled with heroes and helpers.

Perhaps some of us grew up with plenty of adult figures who achieved what they wanted and maintained their integrity in doing it. Perhaps they and others showed us our true abilities and ways to cultivate and express them. But most of us were *not* taken by the hand and led into a lifetime of achieving our best. Most of us have had to find our own heroes and helpers.

A hero is someone who has done something we want to do, who has accomplished something we admire. Remembering that no one is perfect, we can focus on the things we want to emulate in this person, and he or she can serve as our role model. A helper is someone who encourages, nurtures, inspires, and brings out the best in us. We need heroes to see what can be done and helpers to assist us in doing it.

Listening is the beginning of true communication.

Simple communication has become so complicated, confused, and difficult that we often give up on it. We may
start taking it for granted that communication always
means manipulation and deceit. We may not know when
others are being straightforward with us, and we may not
know how to be honest with ourselves. All this complica-
tion and confusion can make communicating with individuals so difficult that we don't even try to communicate
with groups or larger communities.

But we can overcome our fears and uncertainties. We
can communicate openly and honestly on all levels and
with all others. We can begin by *listening*, the most important element of communication. When we're not wrapped
up in getting our point across, we suddenly discover our
own connection to others, our *relationship* with them.
Listen to another person, a baby, a tree, a squirrel, or a
thunderstorm . . . just *listen*.

I share in the world's joy.

The word *compassion* literally means to suffer with others, but only if we define *passion* as suffering and pain. There is another kind of passion. We can be passionate about love, work, people, animals, or the earth. We can enjoy the passion of good health, happiness, and the love of other people. We can passionately accomplish some lofty goals and higher purposes.

We can put our passion anywhere we choose to. A social or political cause, volunteer work, caring for our families, helping others, or learning a specific subject are all things we can be passionate about. Sharing the passion of humanity and the world means not only sharing the sorrow, but also the joy; sharing not just the pain, misery, and want, but also the love, happiness, and infinite abundance.

For one day, I will do no harm to any animal.

We may go through our daily lives without knowing the effects we're having on the animal world, believing our use of animals is unavoidable and necessary for our survival. But if we take just one day to think about the effects everything we do has on animals, we may be surprised.

Buddhist monks who live in the mountains of Tibet don't have access to any form of protein other than the flesh of animals during the winter months. As an offering of thanks, these monks keep animals in their monastery and take good care of them for their entire natural lives. This is a symbolic gesture of *awareness*. They still have to eat meat, but they do what they can to make up for it to the animal world.

We can spend one day thinking about our effects on animals: we can eat lower on the food chain, give up our unnecessary animal products, and be kind to all the creatures with whom we share the earth. In just one day, we can learn a lot.

We share the natural world with all other humans.

Humanity is full of diversity of all kinds—politics, economics, cultures, and viewpoints. Our history is full of the struggles of conflicting peoples. The evolution of cooperation between nations, genders, ethnic and other groups has been a long and bumpy one. It may seem as if we have far more that tears us apart than brings us together.

But wherever we live, whoever we are, whatever our politics, we all share one thing with all other humans: the planet Earth is our home. This fact can be the starting point for coming together in harmony with a common purpose. We're all dependent upon the earth and its resources; we all breathe air, drink water, live off the land. If we take and use this gift, this opportunity to cooperate peacefully for the good of us all, perhaps we can begin moving on to other levels of connectedness and harmony. We have to start somewhere.

*The more I learn about the world, the better my interactions
with it will be.*

Education is our first step toward improving all our
actions. Whether we learn from courses, books, experiences, or other people, everything we learn can help us
improve the world and our effects on it. Whether we learn
individually or collectively, all learning helps stretch
humanity beyond its past mistakes.

H. G. Wells wrote, "Human history becomes more and
more a race between education and catastrophe." We now
know of so many potentially catastrophic problems in the
world that it may seem overwhelming. But everything we
learn, every forward step we take with our true understanding, can change the way we think and act, and that will
change the world. We can begin making amends for the
mistakes we've made in the past and stop making the same
ones now and in the future. We can use our uniquely
human capacity to *learn*.

Thanksgiving is a natural part of the cycle of life.

Many of us may have been taught to thank others for gifts and favors we received without really meaning it. We may have celebrated the American holiday of Thanksgiving without remembering its true essence. We may have developed a habit of sending cards or saying thank you simply as social conventions rather than heart-felt expressions of gratitude or appreciation.

But true thanksgiving is not something we have to do without feeling. It is a natural response to mindfulness or true awareness. When we look and really see, listen and truly hear, think and fully understand, thankfulness flows naturally from our open hearts. The cycles of life are amazingly generous, kind, loving, and appropriate, giving us each what we need. When we take a moment to recognize them, the experience can sometimes move us to tears, and always to true thanksgiving.

Our humanity transcends all our differences.

Focusing on our roles in all the different groups to which we each belong, we often forget the one group to which we *all* belong—the whole human family. We can contribute much more to the world when our outlook includes this role.

All the nations of the world are made up of human beings. This truth overrides whatever differences we have in politics, economics, or social structure. *We are all human.* When we begin focusing on ourselves in this light, always thinking of ourselves and others as *humans* first and foremost, we can begin seeing our connections to one another. We can recognize that our differences are superficial and that our kinship goes much deeper.

I identify with all other living things.

Humans often think of animals, plants, and other life forms in human terms. We imagine they think, feel, and see as we do. We pretend they talk to us in our language. Personifying nonhumans in this way can be very helpful in learning to understand our relationship with them. It's more than just a silly metaphor from children's stories—it's a way of seeing ourselves as part of one whole, interconnected world.

Imagine what it's like to be a bird, flying high over the land and water. Picture in your mind the viewpoint of a rainforest or mountain, an island or desert. Try to feel that you're a cloud full of rain or snow, drifting over the earth, or a rock formation at the bottom of the ocean. Imagine that you are water, flowing gently downstream or thundering down a waterfall. Think like a dolphin, playing in the open sea. All these things are part of life on earth, and therefore part of us. Seeing through their eyes can open our own.

I will consciously cause no harm to others, the earth, or the universe.

Many of us find it difficult to imagine ourselves causing harm in the world. But with no ill will or malicious intent, we may inadvertently cause harm to other people, animals, and nature. Becoming conscious of the effects of our choices can enable us to stop contributing to the damage.

We can begin by becoming aware of everything we buy, eat, drink, wear, and use. We can ask ourselves what we are sending out into the world's air, water, land, and consciousness. If we don't know, we can find out. Everything we do has some impact for which we are responsible. We can change our habits to lessen the burden on the earth and to treat other people with compassion. Living as harmlessly as possible, we lessen the total harm done. If enough of us did this, think of the difference it could make.

Compassion is the mark of true strength.

We humans have discovered our ability to conquer and control many forms of life, including one another. We have found weaknesses in those whom we see as "different" and learned how to exploit them. We have discovered the power we can have over people, animals, air, land, and water.

Now that we know so much about the possibilities of our power, we can turn our attention to the questions of its use. Exactly *how* should we exercise our power, if at all? Just because we *can* do something, does that mean we *should* do it? Matthew Fox writes, "It is the way we treat the weak, be they human or animal, that is the ultimate test of a civilization." Are we civilized enough to treat all others with respect and care? Are we ready to discover the true power and strength in compassion?

Diversity is natural in the universe and in humanity.

Human beings can sometimes be very resistant to diversity. Someone with a different viewpoint may make us question our own, and that may make us feel uncomfortable. Diverse opinions, viewpoints, and ways of living may create great fear and strain within ourselves. We seem to gravitate toward that which is familiar to us.

But even in our own families there is a great deal of diversity. Everyone doesn't have the same talents, abilities, interests, fears, doubts, or passions. Just as the diversity of mountains, oceans, and prairies; lions, caterpillars, and dolphins; and pines, redwoods, and maple trees are all necessary for the earth's ecosystem, the diversity within humanity is a *positive* feature of it. Peace comes from harmony between many diverse parts of one great whole.

REFLECTIONS
ON
MYSELF
& MY
COMMUNITIES

A good man is a public good.

—Robert Augros
George Stanciu

We are social beings. We each belong to a variety of communities. Our families, neighborhoods, towns, cities, or suburbs are some of our primary communities. Our churches, schools, places of employment, and fields of work also create communities in which we participate. We all belong to gender and ethnic groups, political, national, and global communities.

Discovering our relationships and responsibilities to these various communities broadens our self-image. Consciously behaving as a responsible member of a group reveals abilities we may never have known we had and contributions we may never have known we could make.

When we become aware of all the groups to which we belong and then examine our role in each group, we learn what we can do. After turning inward to discover the treasure within us, we turn outward to share that treasure with all the communities in which we live. We do this not only because our communities need our contributions, but also because we each need to make them.

I am a responsible and important citizen of my country.

We in democratic societies have certain rights and responsibilities. Our freedoms require respect and self-control. Our rights require responsible use. Democracy demands a great deal of its citizens. We're supposed to be educated and informed enough to elect our leaders and public servants. We're expected to be self-controlled enough to exercise our rights without violating other people's. We're asked to participate in our government by voting and keeping in touch with our elected representatives.

The price of democracy is not more than we can handle. We can find out how our government works and participate in our own way. We can respect our freedoms enough to use them *responsibly*, taking care not to harm others or ourselves. We can remember how important we each are to the whole country.

I have pride in myself as a positive, contributing energy in the universe.

What does it mean to have pride in ourselves, our nationality, race, gender, ethnicity, or species? Does it mean we see ourselves as *different, better, separate from,* or *dominant over* others? Does it mean that we are *right* and all others are *wrong*? Does it mean that any person or life form who isn't in our group is automatically our *enemy* or at least a lesser being, seen as an object to be exploited? Does pride in ourselves always have to mean power over or contempt for another?

Our healthy self-image includes seeing ourselves as *human,* which makes it impossible for us to hate or harm any other humans. It also includes the knowledge that we are part of an infinite living system, which makes it necessary for us to honor and respect *all* life forms. These beliefs give us pride and self-love and allow us to be a positive, contributing force within humanity and toward the earth and the universe.

The world is a complex and harmonious network.

In business, *networking* helps us cooperate with others whose cooperation we might need at another time. It gives us opportunities for advancement in our field and creates a system in which businesses and individuals can help one another succeed.

In nature, all of life is one big network. Each species helps the others. Every part of the system benefits from and contributes to the whole. If one member of this network has a serious problem or makes a major mistake, the others are affected and the network breaks down. As the one species with the gifts of consciousness and choice, we are responsible for holding up our part of the system, for keeping the network intact. With this responsibility in mind, we can learn to live harmoniously within the network, contribute our share, and receive its abundant benefits.

My life is an important and necessary part of the world.

At some time, we each ask ourselves what our place or purpose is in life. We wonder what difference it makes that we exist, what our role is in the larger scheme of things. We question whether it's worth the trouble to work hard at our lives, to learn all we can, to grow into the best person we can possibly be. The contribution we make compared to all our efforts may seem very small.

But all large, important things are made up of many small, seemingly insignificant parts. Every person is part of the world, of human history, of the energy of the planet and the universe. If we give up our opportunity to positively contribute, we give up on ourselves, our families, our groups and communities, our country, and our world—and the whole universe suffers a loss. Instead, we can simply accept that we may not have the ability to fully understand the meaning of our particular life. We can simply live as if it matters . . . and it will.

I live in society for the good of all.

We live in society with one another because together we can accomplish so much more than we can individually. Together, we can benefit from the educational, financial, and spiritual achievements of others. We can grow in wisdom and well-being because of our community with other people.

All the major religions of all times and places have viewed all people of the world as one great family. We are part and parcel of one another. The objective of living together in society is to harmonize our efforts for our mutual benefit. But human unity doesn't mean the end of diversity any more than unity in nature means that all living things must be pine trees. There is plenty of room for all kinds of talents, abilities, and viewpoints. In fact, such diversity is *essential* for creating the best possible world. Together, our differences can blend into one harmonious whole, for the highest good of all.

I belong to a changing variety of groups.

As we grow through various experiences, we belong to many different groups. At different times, we are members of schools, sports teams, places and fields of work; churches, clubs, or other organizations; cities, neighborhoods, houses, or apartment buildings. We may serve on committees or contribute time and money to various charities or causes. At any given time in our lives, we belong to a unique set of groups and communities.

While we have certain responsibilities to each of these groups, we are also responsible for allowing ourselves to leave them when the time is right for us. Our continued growth and well-being require us to resist getting stuck in one place. Whether it's a job, a residence, or any organization or group, awareness and understanding of our evolving membership enable us to know when—and if—the time comes to move on. Our changing groups reflect our changing and growing selves.

I have the courage to follow my own inner values.

Sometimes we don't act in accordance with our values for a variety of reasons. We may fear drawing attention to ourselves by being different. We may be unsure of our viewpoint, or we may simply lack self-confidence.

It's easy to fall into the groove of doing whatever seems to get the most support—or the least resistance—from others. But inside, we always know when we have gone against our true inner values. It may seem difficult at first, but asking hard questions that challenge conventional practices that are socially or environmentally harmful can become a new habit for us. Is our company, community, or group being socially responsible? Our questioning this can open the door for other people who may have been afraid too.

I am a conscious and conscientious consumer.

One of the most powerful ways we affect our communities is through the things we buy. Our choices of shops, businesses, products, and services significantly influence the larger community. Our purchase is, in effect, an endorsement of a product and the company that produces and sells it. Boycotts have long been used as effective ways to eliminate harmful practices and products from the market.

Every time we are faced with the decision of whether or not to buy a product from a company, we have the power to make a difference. We don't have to support companies that pollute or discriminate. We don't have to buy products that are harmful to people, animals, or the environment. All we have to do is ask a few questions to find out which businesses and products we *want* to support. Then we can support them, avoid the rest, and use our power as consumers to improve all our communities.

Cooperation can benefit all diverse people and groups.

We humans divide ourselves up into *pro-this* and *anti-that* armies, constantly fighting one another. We close ourselves off from communication with our "enemies" rather than trying to understand each others' viewpoints. We forget that the good of all is served by getting together, not pulling apart.

Diversity is good and even necessary; various viewpoints can help round out our knowledge and understanding of any topic. But our insistence on an adversarial method of trying to resolve problems only ends up harming us all. Instead, we can enter into discussions and decision making with an open mind and heart, without seeing those who disagree with us as our enemies but rather as diverse parts of one cohesive group. We can let go of our false assumption that there must always be a *winner* and a *loser*, and instead understand that we can *all* benefit from a positive joint effort.

I allow my identity to grow.

Growth involves change, but change is often hard for us to accept. When we let our identity change, it means we have to let go of some familiar landmarks. We have to stretch some of the boundaries of our own personal worlds. This can make us feel fearful and confused for a while. But as we grow through the process, we find our new identity is an expanded one—a bigger, more inclusive, and more positive one.

We can let self-awareness grow through all the groups we are part of. We can see ourselves as an effective, integral part of many diverse groups. We can outgrow our small, fearful outlook and learn to see ourselves connected to much larger systems. And this new perspective can change our lives.

Whatever happens to the world, happens to me.

We are affected by everything that occurs all over the world. Whether or not we realize it, we are hurt when anyone suffers, hungry when anyone starves, cold when anyone shivers in the night, homeless. We are also uplifted, nourished, and relieved whenever anyone anywhere is helped, healed, sheltered, or fed. Everything that happens, happens to us.

If we doubt that we are so affected by everything, we need only imagine how it would change us and our lives if the world were different. If everyone felt safe, secure, valued, and loved; if they knew they would always have a home and enough to eat; if education, art, music, and nature were free for everyone to enjoy, how different *everything* would be. Contributing whatever we can outside of ourselves contributes to our own safety, happiness, and well-being.

Whatever happens to me, happens to the world.

Taking care of ourselves is a contribution we can all make. It can only help the whole if the parts of that whole are healthy, happy, and functioning in top form. Our well-being can be our greatest gift to humanity.

But sometimes we get confused about what it means to take care of ourselves, to focus on our true well-being. It *doesn't* mean being selfish or inconsiderate, or indulging our every wish and whim. It *does* mean concentrating on our health, safety, and security, and respecting and caring for our body, mind, emotions, and spirit. This gives the world one more person with enough self-love to love other people, animals, green life, the earth, and the universe.

I let go of blaming and focus on doing my part to affect the world positively.

It's easy to become outraged and self-righteous, pointing the finger of blame at everyone else for all the world's problems. But in our defensiveness, are we forgetting to do our part? Maybe we aren't personally responsible for a big company spilling massive amounts of pollutants into the air and water, but do we buy that company's products? What do we send down the drains in our own home? What gases come out of our cars? Do we drive them unnecessarily? We can all do more to help clean up, conserve, and maintain the delicate balance of the earth's natural resources.

Blaming doesn't get anything done. Becoming aware of all the effects *we* have on the world and consciously making them positive ones will.

My work reflects one of my best contributions to the world.

If we let ourselves get stuck in a job we hate, one that doesn't make use of our best abilities and talents or makes us go against our inner sense of truth, we suffer for it. If we let ourselves get caught complaining and feeling resentful about our work, we can't do our best.

We need to infuse our work with our best selves and our highest viewpoint. We can refuse to let negativity get to us and make us waste opportunities for doing work that we love, work that makes use of our talents and contributes positively to the world. We need to open our mind to what we *can* do. Finding and performing our *right livelihood* is one of the most important ways we can help improve the world.

REFLECTIONS ON MYSELF & THE EARTH

*Together with the sea, air, sunlight, and other life forms, we
take part in a planet-sized living system.*
—Elizabeth Roberts

As conscious—and *self*-conscious—beings on this planet,
we are in a unique position to affect it. We have har-
nessed electricity, using it for light, heat, and other purposes. We have found natural substances for healing. We
are beginning to understand nature's ability to heal our dis-
tressed minds with aromas, sounds, and visual beauty.

We can cause great damage to natural systems, but we
can stop the harm, and often, reverse it. We can walk
lightly on the earth, deliberately becoming a positive link
in the life chain, contributing our awareness and action to
improve life for all species.

As we grow in our awareness of our place in the complex
web of life, we learn to take less and give more back. We
start to think of ourselves as connected to all living things.
We begin to feel our way to a balanced, harmonious life.
We're part of a beautiful living system, but we must use our
human capabilities to their fullest. Taking care of the earth
for ourselves and future generations is life-affirming and
self-affirming. The earth is not just our home, it's *us*.

Everything grows and evolves in cycles.

The natural rhythm of life is cyclical. The sun, the moon, the seasons, the development of nations, relationships, and people all go through never-ending cycles. Sometimes we become impatient with this, wishing the cycles of our lives and world would stop in one place. In our linear thinking, we may feel frustrated or even angry with the sense of always taking two steps forward and one step back.

Understanding the cyclical nature of all life can help us to accept these natural cycles and grow with them. We can learn to recognize all the cycles, large and small, of our lives and of all life around us. We can stop resisting the constant ebb and flow of life and learn instead to trust it. We can harmonize all of our efforts and choices with life's natural rhythm and begin fully experiencing, appreciating, and even enjoying every twist and curve.

I am not a user of the earth, but a responsible part of it.

Many of us were taught to see the earth as a big, limitless supermarket for human beings to use. The plants, minerals, gases, water, and animals that flourish here are all seen as toys or objects for human survival. We have forgotten our place in the natural order of the planet.

As the only beings with our level of consciousness on the earth, we are capable of a great deal of manipulation of all the other life forms. We are also capable of making destructive, and, ultimately, self-destructive, choices in these interactions. But if we change our self-image from a dominant user to an integral part of the whole life system, we can begin contributing our consciousness, and all that it is capable of, to the maintenance and betterment of all life. Our human gifts don't give us despotic rule over the earth, but responsibility for it.

Nature surrounds me, wherever I am.

Many of us live in large urban communities filled with concrete and steel. We may think that nature is far from us, out in the country somewhere, and we can't get to it.

But nature is everywhere, all around us, all the time. It's not just found in our dogs, cats, and potted plants. When we look at concrete, we can think about the sand, gravel, and water that went into it. When we see houses and furniture, we can remember the trees that gave us that wood. When we put on our clothes and make our bed, we can think of the cotton plants, the woolly sheep, and the downy geese that contributed to our warmth and comfort.

The natural world is all around us. Metals and precious gems are mined from the earth. Even many plastics come from petroleum products, which come from crude oil. Everything, everywhere, is part of one whole natural world. We can see it, think about it, and remember that we're part of it too.

The earth nourishes me and keeps me alive.

Because it passes through so many hands and processes from its original state to our dinner plates, we often forget where our food really comes from—the earth. We live in a continuous cycle of using and replenishing nature. If we're careful not to waste and to always replenish the earth, if we share what we have and remember its source, the earth will provide all we need—for all of us.

When we eat, we can think about the cows that gave us milk, cheese, yogurt, and ice cream; the chickens that gave us eggs; the birds and beasts that gave us their own flesh; the plants and trees that provide us with the grains, fruits, nuts, and vegetables we live on. This planet is uniquely suited to providing all we need to live and flourish. And we—with our large brains—are uniquely suited to taking care of, respecting, replenishing, and thanking the earth.

I listen to what the earth can teach me.

The earth is our classroom. It can teach us everything we need to know about life, the universe, and ourselves. It can show us unity, diversity, equality, peace, harmony, beauty, growth, rest, death, and rebirth. It can teach us patience, generosity, tolerance, forgiveness, and perseverance. It can help us understand the power of surrendering to its natural rhythms and the joy of accepting its natural course.

The earth is our mother. She can give us everything we need to survive, grow, and flourish. She can tell us who we are and help us see our potential. She shows us the way but doesn't force us to follow it. She lets us make mistakes, expecting that, eventually, we will learn.

Everything in nature has a purpose.

Sometimes we human beings seem more like bulldozers on the earth rather than members of the community of life. We tear down, push aside, bore through, and cross over much of the planet, but do we really *see* it? The earth is an amazingly complex and harmonious organism, full of countless small parts, each doing their bit to keep the whole alive.

But we humans often see nature as a nuisance, something to overcome, dominate, control, and conquer. Rather than recognize our part in the whole glorious scheme, we fear the energy of nature. Seeing ourselves as the center of the universe, we view every rainfall, drought, and forest fire only in terms of what it can do *to us*. We see it as a force that can mess up our plans. But the truth is, nature is always performing perfectly. Everything it does is correct and appropriate. If we simply learn to harmonize with its natural energy, it will take care of us.

I am loyal to all life, to the planet Earth, and to the universe.

Author E. B. White wrote, "It is easier for a man to be loyal to his club than to his planet; the bylaws are shorter, and he is personally acquainted with the other members." The bylaws of living on the earth do seem to be many and complex. We have found ourselves breaking them and suffering the consequences before we even knew what we were doing. Not being personally acquainted with the other members of the living family makes it easy for us to ignore, neglect, vilify, hate, and destroy one another.

Loyalty to humanity, other life forms, and the earth is no longer an amusing impossibility, but a requirement for our survival. Environmental devastation and the threat of nuclear war bind us all inextricably together. Whether we collectively sink or swim depends on our own choices.

The earth can provide plenty for everyone.

Sometimes we forget the ability of the earth to provide all the food, water, minerals, and other essentials we need. We think that there is scarcity and lack, that some must suffer so that others can have what they need. But the earth is plentiful enough for *all of us*. Scarcity only *appears* to occur because of our methods of distribution, economics, and politics. The earth doesn't pick and choose who may drink her water or eat her fruits—*we* do.

When we begin seeing ourselves as interconnected beings, we realize that, ultimately, we are all harmed by our complicated system wherein some have nothing and others have far more than they need. How *obvious* it is that there is enough for everyone, if only we'd see it that way. How *simple* it would be to just grow all that the earth offers us and share it freely. How *easy* it is for those of us who have enough to give some of it away.

*I use my human power to harmonize with and appreciate
nature.*

Many of us were taught that humanity was given *dominion* over the earth. And it does seem clear that we humans have the intellectual and physical ability to overpower nature in many ways. Unfortunately, we often interpret this to mean that we have the right to use everything in nature in any way we wish, without regard for the consequences.

Humanity is dependent upon nature, and this means that our use of nature must be benevolent or we will lose our very source of life. We cannot abuse nature and expect it to continue providing us with everything we need to survive. We can't perpetually take from the earth without caring for its needs and replenishing it. We can't separate our own fate from the fate of the planet. If we humans have a unique power over the earth, we can choose to use that power either to destroy ourselves or to contribute our gifts for the betterment of all life.

Nature provides us with beautiful scents.

One of the ways nature communicates with us is through scent. Foul odors warn us of spoiled food and pollutants in our air and water. But nature is also filled with scents we humans find beautiful, soothing, exciting, and comforting. Lilacs and roses, cinnamon and mint, fruits and herbs, the earthy scent of soil and greenery, and the fresh clean scent of seaside air are only a few of the many wonderful aromas the earth offers us.

Sometimes we fill our environments with so many artificial perfumes that we forget the natural scents abundant in nature. We forget the simple, natural pleasure of smelling apples, oranges, peaches, roses, sage, pine, freshly hewn wood, or newly cut grass. But we can always find these and many other pleasing scents in nature. We can visit them in their natural settings or bring them into our daily environments. Doing this regularly can help us stay close to nature and enjoy one of its most beautiful gifts.

I see beauty everywhere in nature.

Beauty is inherent in nature. Without any training or education in art or the principles of color and form, people always, everywhere, describe nature's beauty. Waterfalls, rainbows, sunsets, and skies full of stars inspire us to poetry. Mountains, canyons, and giant redwood trees take our breath away. A soft twilight snowfall fills us with peace.

No one had to teach us that blazing sunsets were beautiful. We didn't have to study meteorology or geology to be fascinated by rainbows and canyons. Our response to the beauty in nature is as natural as the beauty itself. It strikes a chord deep within us. It reminds us of how wonderful, how amazing, how beautiful the world truly is. It reawakens our natural love for the earth and the universe. There is a theory that nature makes human and animal babies *cute* to the adult species so that we'll take care of them. How much more magnificent would the earth have to be before we'd take better care of it?

The energy of the universe is infinite.

We are taught early in school that nothing can be created or destroyed, but can only change form. Acorns can become trees, trees can become houses, tables, sawdust, or paper. Even the smoke and gases from a wood fire go out into the atmosphere in some form and continue to exist. Everything is part of an infinite continuum.

We often lose touch with this sense of eternity because of the comings and goings of our own part in the process. But the water in our faucet doesn't originate there any more than our trash ceases to exist when we put it out. We can reconnect with the infinity of life by asking ourselves, *Where did this come from?* and *Where is this going?* about everything we use. We can remember the infinite connections between everything that exists and the unending chain of life. We can consciously make our little bit of the continuum as positive and helpful to the whole as possible.

*Ecological imbalance is the result of human imbalance
on a personal and social level.*

The environmental problems we are now facing on a global scale are a reflection of our unresolved personal and social problems. Our difficulties in loving and communicating with ourselves and each other create difficulties in relating to nature in a harmless and harmonious way. It all comes down to our basic beliefs about who we are and what our role is in the whole scheme of things.

When we begin recognizing and nurturing our physical, intellectual, emotional, spiritual, and social selves, we learn that taking our rightful place of responsibility within nature is a way of taking care of ourselves. When we begin resolving our personal and social errors, we develop a more positive relationship with nature. When we start working in earnest on our most intimate relationships, we become better able to deal effectively with larger and larger communities, and ultimately, the whole world.

Nature fills me with humility.

Discovering our place within the infinite living system of the universe reminds us that many of the things we think are important simply aren't. Our daily lives, so full of superficial details, busy activities, and concerns, seem almost insignificant in the context of all of humanity, the world, and even the universe. With all our modern technology, knowledge, and power, we still can't create a single mountain or ocean, nor can we cure many diseases.

Our humility when faced with nature's power and beauty doesn't tell us that we're insignificant little cogs in a great massive living system, but rather that we are *very important* little cogs. When we learn to work in harmony with nature rather than fight against it, we can discover the power and joy of being an integral part of it. We can turn our attention to what's really important and make our impact on nature a positive—or at least a harmless—one.

I am grateful for the gift of fire.

Imagine a world without fire. Our ancestors would not have survived the cold or have been able to cook their food without it. We're used to seeing it now only in a controlled state. In its natural state, we often find it destructive and frightening.

Fire, like all forms of energy in the universe, *can* be destructive. It can transform trees, houses, and the bodies of living things into ash. It can injure us, take away our possessions, and leave us destitute. But fire can also comfort us, heal us, give us heat, and sustain our lives. It can even give us the warm, primal feelings of a campfire or a cozy hearth. We can respect fire as a precious natural gift.

Water sustains all life.

Through the gift of water, all life is nourished and sustained. Without it, the trees would die, our food wouldn't grow, animals wouldn't survive, and we humans—our bodies consisting mostly of water—couldn't live. And yet we take for granted that water will always be plentiful for us, clean and nourishing, no matter what we do.

Like fire, water must be treated with respect for its true nature, with appreciation for its gifts, and with care for its continued abundance. Like everything in the universe, water cannot be destroyed, but it can be transformed into lifeless poison. Mistreating this precious gift is harmful to all life. We can use our human gifts of consciousness and ingenuity to change our ways of seeing and treating the life-giving gift of water.

Music is a gift of nature.

Nature provides us with a constant symphony of beautiful sounds. Water and air, birds and animals, trees and other plants fill the world with music. The patter of gentle rain, the rhythmic thunder of the seashore, the rustling of leaves and crackling of fire all serenade us with the song of life. The melodies of birds, whales, and wolves comfort us with nature's lullaby.

We humans also contribute our voices and the sounds of all the instruments we have invented to the orchestra. Since the beginning of time, we have chanted, sung, hummed, and created everything from wind chimes to violins to electric pianos. Listening to the sounds of all nature, including our own beautiful music, can help us feel happy, calm, peaceful, and healed. We can always turn to the gift of music; it is here for every one of us to enjoy.

Every inch of space is part of the infinite living universe.

There is no place in the universe where absolutely *nothing* exists. And yet, we often think of so much of the earth and the universe as *nothingness*. If we learn to look more closely, using our mind and not just our eyes, we can begin seeing all kinds of wonderful, miraculous *stuff* everywhere.

Science helps us to see more of this stuff than we can actually perceive with our eyes. We know that there are such things as atoms and molecules, germs and bacteria. We know that the atmosphere is filled with transparent gases and that sound produces invisible *waves* in the air. Perceiving all the hidden *things* in apparently empty space can help us understand the interconnectedness of everything in the universe. We can begin to sense the underlying energy that is present everywhere, the glue that holds the entire universe together as one whole living system.

Surrounded by nature, I feel my connection with it.

When we place ourselves in a natural setting, we feel different. Away from the sights, scents, and sounds of busy streets and neighborhoods, we come into closer contact with the natural world. Surrounded by plants, trees, grasses, sand, soil, water, and rocks, we remember our basic harmony with nature.

Standing barefoot on a beach, watching the sea, hearing the waves, breathing the air, we forget the busy cares of our everyday lives. In the middle of a forest, sheltered by tall trees, serenaded by birds and rustling leaves, we become one with them. Climbing a hill, rock, or mountain, our perspective changes radically. As Ralph Waldo Emerson wrote, "Standing on the bare ground, all mean egotism vanishes . . . the currents of the Universal Being circulate through me." Surrounded by nature, we discover our spiritual selves, our natural selves, our real selves.

Whatever we do to the earth, we do to ourselves.

It's easy to get caught up in all kinds of theories and arguments about our responsibilities to the natural world. It's easy to see only as far as what seems to harm or benefit us in the short term. But while we're busy arguing, our actions are creating consequences in the world. While we're distracted with questions of who's right and who's wrong, the earth is suffering under the weight of our confusion.

Turning our need to figure out how we should live in this world into a war between businesses and environmentalists, government and people, or humans and other life forms only puts off the ultimate solutions and makes them harder to achieve. In some cases, the time we waste makes the decisions for us. But we don't have to waste any more time arguing with one another. We can begin to understand that the fate of the earth is *our* fate and stop self-destructing.

I close my eyes and imagine that I am a tree.

Standing on the earth, I am an integral part of it. My roots reach deep down into the land, firmly anchored in rock, sand, and soil. The nourishing water I find with my roots circulates throughout my body, energizing me. My feet cling to the earth as it spins gently through space.

My trunk stands straight and tall, strong and solid. My arms reach out in all directions, softly bending with the breeze. I sway back and forth, slowly, without breaking. My fingers stretch out, fluttering, caressing the wind. I drink in the green air and light, and sighing, give it back.

Whispering, I call to the birds and squirrels, my sweet family, *Come home, nestle in my arms.* We rock together on the breath of life. I look out over the land, feeling the wind whistle through my hair, and turning my face up toward the sun, I kiss the sky.

I take a moment every day to remember my true place.

Forgetting who we truly are leads us to make many mistakes and creates many problems in the world. If we lose sight of our highest potential, we can't live up to it. If we focus all our attention on the superficial details of life, we'll neglect to contribute to the overall well-being of ourselves and the world. If we don't take the time to step back and remember, we won't see the forest for the trees.

While the trees—the everyday choices we have to make—are important, we can always take better care of them by keeping the whole forest in mind. Decisions become clearer and easier with a constant understanding of the wider implications and consequences of our actions. Just a moment each day can keep us mindful of our true importance in the world, our effectiveness, and our responsibilities. It can change everything.

I value all life in the universe.

Sometimes we think we value something, but we don't act as if we do. We may rationalize away our inconsistencies and choose to live with vague feelings of doubt and confusion. But when our actions and choices reflect our highest values, the result is the contentment of living effectively and consistently.

We may go through our lives missing the many opportunities to connect on a conscious level with all forms of living energy. We may use the products supplied by land, minerals, water, plants, and animals without ever thinking about, conserving, or thanking them. We may even forget that other people are expressions of this life force and treat them carelessly. If we truly value life, we value all its forms and expressions, and we will treat them *all* with care, respect, and love—including ourselves.

I have a reciprocal relationship with nature.

Many of us habitually *reciprocate* for favors and gifts we receive. If someone has us over to their house for dinner, we invite them over to ours at another time. If someone baby-sits or house-sits for us or does an errand for us, we do the same for them when they need help. When people support us in our efforts, encourage us to do our best, cheer for our successes and comfort us in our defeats, we try to be there for them in the same ways.

But how often do we think to *reciprocate* for the food we eat, the air we breathe, the clothes we wear, the buildings we live in, or the water we use to drink, cook, and wash? Do we feel honored and grateful for these generous gifts? Do we remember where these things come from? We can give back to the earth through conserving, recycling, and living as a close friend and relative to it.

Nature is infinitely reliable.

While change is constant in every area of life, nature can be counted on to perform in a consistent and reliable way. Spring follows winter, rain comes from clouds, and greenery gives us oxygen to breathe. Nature doesn't let us down. As poet Wendell Berry writes, "Put your faith in the two inches of humus that will build under the trees every thousand years."

Without human interference, the earth will take care of itself and all its life forms. When nature seems to let us down, it is truly ourselves who have erred by either interfering with the earth's natural rhythms or choosing to view a natural event as a problem or disaster. When we look at the world from a more natural viewpoint, all its activities make sense.

I leave the earth untouched as much as possible.

Henry David Thoreau wrote, "In Wildness is the preservation of the World." The areas of the earth that are left completely alone and untouched by humans live, grow, and contribute their proper part to the whole. The rainforests, oceans, mountains, deserts, and plains all perform in harmony to keep the whole earth in balance.

The more we affect the earth and all its natural cycles, the less whole and healthy it becomes. Areas of "wildness" are necessary and healthful for the planet and for us. Besides carefully avoiding damaging the earth by the products we use and the things we eat and do, we can contribute to the natural wildness of the planet in our own small ways. We can let a little patch of garden grow wild in our own backyard; we can watch it and see what grows there, what the earth does on its own. We can think twice before cutting down trees or paving over any area of land. We can leave parts of the earth untouched.

I can learn from the plants and animals.

Focused only on ourselves, we often forget how much we can learn from the natural world. Impressed and obsessed with our own unique capacities, we may neglect to notice all the things plant and animal life can teach us. Blinded by our own particular viewpoint, we may not take advantage of their lessons.

D. H. Lawrence wrote, "I never saw a wild thing sorry for itself." From plants and animals we can learn patience, acceptance, perseverance, and generosity. They fulfill their purpose in life without all our angst and resistance. They rise in the morning singing and gather together in the evening to quietly watch the sun set in the sky. They work tirelessly and play with abandon. They find the tiniest ray of sunshine and grow toward the light. We can all learn to be a little bit more like plants and animals.

What is good for the earth is good for me.

So often we forget that taking care of the natural world is not self-sacrifice or deprivation. In fact, it's self-serving for humans to care for animals, plant life, water, land, and air. We have made some mistakes along the way, while thinking we were doing good for ourselves. But now we recognize the damage we have done to the earth's natural rhythms. We can still use our desire to take care of ourselves by learning how to truly take care of the earth.

When we recycle, we do it to make a better, healthier environment for ourselves. When we bicycle or walk instead of using a car, we breathe air that's a little bit cleaner. When we conserve energy, we save money and cause a little less waste of the earth's resources—which means there'll be more for us and our children later. When we take care of the earth, we're taking care of ourselves.

I am one with the whales of the sea.

I swim the endless ocean waves, floating, diving, singing. In my heavenly playground, without a care, I welcome the sun and clouds alike. I dive beneath the waves to the cool dark deep, calling to my friends and relations, the sound of my voice as deep and cool as the water. And bursting out again into the sun, I sing the total and complete joy of life.

Gathered together, my children's sweet voices rise, echoing my own. They circle around, laughing, playing, joyful simply in *being*. Together we watch, looking all around us at infinity. We see farther than the ends of the earth. We drink and breathe and live the electric pulse of the living earth, the heartbeat of all life, everywhere. And we cannot help but sing.

The energy of the universe is within me.

The same energy that turns the earth on its axis and spins it around the sun moves through us. The energy of earthquakes, hurricanes, and erupting volcanos lives within us. The vibrancy of mountain lions, grizzly bears, and ocean tides pulses in our hearts. The energy of the universe lives and breathes through us.

This energy may sometimes seem frightening or destructive, but only when we misinterpret it or get in the way of its natural course. When we try to control it by force rather than understand it, the energy may be interrupted. When our negative attitudes get in the way, our energy may get stuck or misdirected. But when we accept the goodness of the flow of energy, we can begin letting it do its good work unimpeded. We can become a clear, open conduit for the powerful, loving, and creative energy of the universe.

I am part of healing the whole world.

It is not news to us that the world needs healing. On all levels—personal, social, national and international, environmental and global—the world is wounded, sick, and worn out. But the process of healing is natural in the universe and has already begun. Every one of us is part of it. We can contribute every aspect of our lives to the healing of the earth and her people.

Everything we think, say, and do has ripple effects from here to infinity. Every choice we make affects the whole world. This seems an awesome responsibility, but one we can rise to and meet with our unique human capabilities. The challenge before us is to heal ourselves, one another, all the plant and animal life, and the whole earth. The responsibility is to ourselves and all future generations. What a wonderful opportunity to spend our lives in the highest purpose imaginable—*healing*.

115

I am like a mountain.

Mountains stand tall, strong, and solid. Unmoving, they withstand rain, snow, wind, and fire. They give shelter and life to countless plants and animals, trees and wildflowers, without judging whether they deserve it or not. They stand where they have stood for millions of years, where they will stand for millions of years to come, peacefully looking out over the land and sea. They don't fight the passage of time or the changes it brings. They don't block the life pulsing endlessly through them or tire of meeting each new day. Taking their time, they heal yesterday's wounds without worrying about tomorrow.

We can be like the mountain, think like the mountain. We can love generously and enjoy serenity like the mountain. We can flourish in our cool, dark shadows and deep caves, as well as glory in the bright light of our summit. We can look out over the land and sea and know that everything is good.

I pledge allegiance to the earth
and all its forms and expressions of life;
to all my brothers and sisters
the human family
plants
animals
mountains
oceans
prairies
and streams.
I pledge to protect the safety and sanctity
of my mother, the earth
my father, the sky
my brother, the sun
my sister, the moon
and all my relations throughout the universe.
I pledge to cause no harm
and to do good wherever and whenever I can;
to be mindful
in all my interactions.
I pledge allegiance to my self,
as part and parcel
of the whole;
one world
indivisible
with respect and compassion
for all.

Resources to support personal change…

Trusting Intuition
by Helene Lerner-Robbins
Trust yourself. You can have faith in your personal and spiritual progress. These innovative new meditation books bolster your self-confidence and affirm that you are where you need to be in your recovery journey.

My Timing Is Always Right
There are no coincidences and no mistakes. You are in the right place in your recovery. Overcome worry and anxiety about the frustrations of daily situations. Discover why people, places, and things are as they should be—right now—in your life. 96 pp.   Order No. 5471

Embrace Change
When old ways no longer work and new behaviors feel uncomfortable, *Embrace Change*. These affirmations and meditations help you make the most of the day and focus on the future. Find renewed courage for making changes in your attitudes, ideas, projects, and relationships. 96 pp.   Order No. 5470

Choosing Happiness
The Art of Living Unconditionally
by Veronica Ray
Are you living "conditionally"? Limited by ifs and buts in your enjoyment of life? With constant encouragment Veronica Ray gives you the framework for maintaining a positive outlook. You *can learn* to create your own happiness in relationships, work situations, financial affairs, and in the face of sudden loss or change. 238 pp.

Order No. 5114

*For price and order information, or a free catalog,
please call our Telephone Representatives.*

HAZELDEN EDUCATIONAL MATERIALS
Pleasant Valley Road • P.O. Box 176
Center City, MN 55012-0176
1-800-328-9000 (Toll Free. U.S., Canada, & the Virgin Islands)
1-612-257-4010 (Outside the U.S. & Canada)
1-612-257-1331 (FAX)

HAZELDEN EUROPE • Cork, Ireland
Int'l Code+ 353+21+314+318